Lessons from a Venetian Vinedresser

Lessons

from a

Venetian

Vinedresser

Robert Scott Stiner

Lessons from a Venetian Vinedresser
by Robert Scott Stiner
Copyright © 2001 by Bridge-Logos Publishers
International Standard Book Number: 0-88270-881-3
Library of Congress Catalog Card Number: 2001096392

Published by:
Bridge-Logos *Publishers*
Gainesville, FL 32614 USA
www.bridgelogos.com

Dedicated to
Rachel
Silas
and
Dannielle

C O N T E N T S

PART THREE
Autumn - *Harvest*

PART FOUR
Winter - *Rest*

PART FIVE

With loving appreciation to:

Aldo, Sarah and Alan Bruzzo,
thank you so much for all those lunches
that most people only dream of.

Otis and Martha Brady
for being examples of branches that grow correctly.

My editor, Sue Morris,
founder of Shakespeare Studio.
How anyone can do as much as you is beyond me.

Maurizio Di Nuovo
for taking me to so many great little
coffee shops around the Veneto Region.

My students at Caserma Ederle
for allowing me to build, paint and stand
on all my soap-boxes for three years.

Keith Green and Rich Mullins
for inspiring me.

And most of all to my amazing wife, Trish.

FOREWORD

A parable or an allegory normally teaches one main truth. There can be a thousand ways to look at a parable and you can gain something from each of those different ways.

But, just as there are a thousand ways to peel an orange, there is still one main objective and that is consuming the fruit.

The one main truth that Christ taught to His disciples in John 15: 1-9, is the necessity to abide or remain in Him in order to bear fruit unto the Father.

I am not writing a definitive work on this allegory, but rather attempting to have you the reader, see in a clearer way our relationship in abiding in our Lord.

Some of these chapters are essays, some are analogies, but all have a common thread that runs through them; they all have touched the heart of the writer as he walked the vineyards of the Veneto region of Italy.

It's hard not to get a sense of the love of God walking through a field throughout the different seasons and watching the clusters of tiny flowers turn into big, juicy fruit. And now let us look at how the taking care of a vineyard relates to the words that Christ spoke and how those words relate to our lives today.

The process and result of our fellowship with Christ is ultimately advancing His Kingdom.

INTRODUCTION

Directions to
Ca'Bruzzo

It's hard to know for sure if you're on the right road the first time you go to Ca'Bruzzo. The autostrada part is quite easy. From Vicenza one has two choices, left to Venice or right to Milan. My directions say "go toward Milan, take the Montebello exit and head toward Lonigo". Once in Lonigo however, everything changes. Like many of the towns in the Veneto region, as you enter, the roads quickly narrow and you feel a heightened sense of awareness as the oncoming traffic just misses your side mirror as they go by, and a little scooter passes you on the other side at the same time.

After traveling through Lonigo, I started the steep climb up the hillside on the winding roads. In only a few kilometers time, a view almost unsurpassed opens before me. First come the images, later would come the words. I pull over off the road to the shoulder and try to take it all in. Standing on a cliff on this clear, crisp

January day, you need your sunglasses, or if you're driving, at least to put the visor down as this riposo sun hides around every other turn up the foothills. Still looking out, my view is bounded by the far-off mountain chain of the Italian Alps with their jagged-toothed snow tips rising toward the heavens, and nearer, the pine-covered hills of Marostica.

Sweeping slightly to the northwest, before Verona, Romeo and Juliet's castle. Nearer yet, my eyes rest here and there on little terra-cotta towns glittering in the sunlight.

Traveling over these romantic hills and glens I find myself in the farmland of vineyards. Around me are rolling fields of the richest fertility, freshly plowed deeper than most, with the richest of loam soils turned for the upcoming season.

But for the most part, I see countless vineyards covering this magnificent land; dipping and rising and winding throughout the hillsides. Every turn is a vineyard connected to the next and all have been put to bed for the long goodnight of winter. Earth tone colored villas and winery farm homes and cantinas are dotted throughout these hills. Four-foot walls of cream-yellow fieldstones follow the topography of the land with every dip and curve that form multi-level terraces and boundaries for the different types of vines.

In the low lying valleys, I see fringes of dense fog laying perfectly still as if to hide from the sun that will soon nudge them to be on their way; and only a few laborers in some of the fields repairing supports for the upcoming season. An old, Italian man on an old farm tractor, with its tires caked in red clay, has just come out of a field and is heading down the narrow road as I am heading up. We both offer part of the road and with a respectful wave to each other, slowly pass. The air in this area seems to have an aroma of hard work and good moral people. A few winding kilometers more, I see a sign for San Germano and under that, Ca'Bruzzo winery. It's hard to know for sure if you're on the right road the first time you go to Ca'Bruzzo, but there are always signs.

John 15:1-9

"I am the true vine, and My Father is the vinedresser
Every branch in Me that does not bear fruit, He takes away;
And every branch that bears fruit, He prunes
it so that it may bear more fruit.
You are already clean because of the word
which I have spoken to you.
Abide in Me, and I in you.
As the branch cannot bear fruit of itself unless it abides in the vine,
so neither can you unless you abide in Me.
I am the vine, you are the branches;
He who abides in Me and I in him,
he bears much fruit,
For apart from Me you can do nothing.
If anyone does not abide in Me, he is thrown away
as a branch and dries up;
And they gather them, and cast them into
the fire and they are burned.
If you abide in Me, and My words abide in you,
ask whatever you wish, and it will be done for you.
By this is my father glorified, that you bear much fruit,
and so prove to be My disciples.
Just as the Father has loved Me,
I have also loved you; Abide in My love"

Jesus Christ

Part One

Spring

Beginning

It's early spring and the brown-gray branches are starting to show the beginnings of life. Where the skeletons of this vast vineyard have endured the long cold winter, green sprouts start to appear as the sun begins to warm the earth. If we had better ears, we could hear the stretching of the new branches out of the old with the vigor and strength of a new season. If we could see in time lapse, we'd see the new branches almost vibrate as they develop nubs that turn into small leaves with tentacles reaching out for something to hold on to.

Some of the branches are following the horizontal patterns of the rows and some are wildly growing out into the center of the aisles. Their concern is simply to grow as far and as fast as they can with the nourishment being provided them.

A few weeks pass and upon taking a closer look at the individual branches, I can see most of them have tiny clusters of white flowers growing. The almost invisible flowers only last a couple of days and then, as they dry, I see in their place tiny green dots.

Chapter 1

Seeing Differently

I had writer's block, trying to work on my book about the miracles of Christ. Some miracles are easy to write about, it's all right there in front of me. The research is fun, too; when I know where to go and what to look for. Then, there was the deaf mute. I loved the story in the Bible, but I couldn't think of that much to write. Time was slowly rolling along and still nothing. I read more, I drank more coffee, looked out the window. I even shot paper wads in the wastepaper basket but still, no inspiration. After awhile I found myself staring at a blinking cursor. I left the office, went out into the yard, and decided to go for a walk. That walk would change my life forever.

Our villa is surrounded with vineyards so it's a great place to walk and relax. It's one of my favorite things to do when I pray or think about things. I walked up the steep ridge behind our home and followed it to a plateau where rows of grapevines go off in all directions. I was going to follow the path I sometimes walk, but at the last minute I decided to look for another route.

I was choosing my new path when I noticed something hanging off the beginning of one of the rows. I walked closer to investigate, wondering if it might be something left in the field by one of the workers from the past harvest. I noticed a small lunch bag sitting on the ground and hanging over one of the vines was an old, dark green wool coat with a wool hat balanced on it. Beside the bag was another bag stuffed full of long, thin, green rubber tubes about the length of a shoestring if you were to take it out of your shoe. Next to that I saw a pair of rubber boots that go over work boots to keep them dry. My first thought was "why would someone be working in the vineyards this time of year?" and then "why is there only one person and what could he possibly be doing?" I was so intrigued that I had to look into this peculiar situation. I didn't see or hear anyone, but thought someone must be close by, so I walked down the row.

The rolling hills obscured my view from seeing very far ahead, but as I walked I heard someone singing and stopped long enough to recognize a man's Italian voice not far ahead of me. I approached with caution. Slowly, I moved into position as if to look at a wild deer before it spots you and leaps off into the forest. Just as I got to the crest of the hill, down the same row and about fifty yards ahead of me, was a man. He didn't see me, so I squatted down and watched him working. He was an Italian man that looked to be in his sixties with silver hair and a few darker traces still left from his younger days. He had on a long sleeve shirt, work pants and boots. Hanging out of his pockets were handfuls of those green rubber tubes and in his hand was a pair of small pruners. He worked alone in this vast vineyard. After watching him for only a few moments, it was as if the Holy Spirit said, "that's the vinedresser".

My mind was reeling with excitement as I watched this man and for the first time I saw John chapter fifteen come alive before my very eyes.

Here was an old man singing to the vines as if to serenade them as he did the work that only he could do. Each branch he touched and ran his fingers along it; inspected and trimmed it in such a way that would cause it to bear the most fruit, the best fruit.

He wasn't in a hurry and the time this process took seemed to be irrelevant to this vinedresser. It was the end product, even if it would still be a long time away, which was of the utmost relevance.

As I watched him, he did things I didn't understand. For example, instead of simply trimming a branch that had grown wildly, sometimes he would carefully weave it back into the pattern of the other branches. Other times he would simply trim them off from the vine. I couldn't understand why some were trimmed and others were woven back in. At the time, my eyes could not see any difference from one branch to the next. It was as if only the vinedresser knew exactly what he was trying to accomplish. He was looking for something that I couldn't see.

The lone worker did something else that was peculiar to me as well. With his pruners in hand, and with every set of branches, he was cutting off the thin, green tubes that were already in place and tying on new ones in the exact spot. All of the branches received the same methodical treatment, but the vinedresser didn't seem to mind as those Italian songs filled the air.

In the rows between the vines lay one continuous pile of branches and the green elastic bands. Other people would come through later to gather them up and discard them into a fire to be burned. It seemed to me that too much was being cut off, so much being wasted. I was sure those branches could have produced plenty of fruit, but then again, the vinedresser knew exactly what he was doing.

Watching this fascinating process, the spiritual truths and applications of what I had seen were far greater than I could take in. So, after making my way back to the house, I started to research the details of these truths.

C h a p t e r   2

Two Types of Vineyards

*A*fter walking through and studying more vineyards than I can possibly remember, I have come to this conclusion: in northern Italy, there are, for the most part, two types of vineyards.

There are what I call the rented vineyard and the family-owned vineyard. First, the rented vineyard is one for which a landowner doesn't do the work himself. He hires laborers to do the different stages of the work involved. These hired hands do a good job, and for the most part, when the trimming is finished the vineyards are esthetically beautiful and as symmetrical as freshly trimmed, brushed cherry hedges on someone's manicured lawn. When all the leaves have matured, they are really something to see, row after row of deep green hedge-like vines and branches.

It doesn't take long for the workers to come through and do the trimming of the branches. Depending on the size of the vineyard, there can be quite a few trimmers. Since the landowner pays for the work rendered, he wants the job done as quickly as possible, which only makes sense if you are running a business. Many of these vineyards at harvest time have the grapes sold off to another producer. This producer ultimately makes the wine. The landowner's goal is to produce as many grapes as possible, because he gets paid by the overall weight of the harvest. In this type of vineyard, nothing gets wasted, as far as the fruit goes. The fruit can be very healthy or sickly. I've even seen some rotten fruit making its way into the wine press. If the landowner has the field as an investment, then the quality of the wine isn't as important as the amount of wine produced.

Now the family-owned vineyard is very different. It is run with a different philosophy and a different purpose. There is only one vinedresser rather than many trimmers. The fruit of the vine will not be resold for processing. The family-owned vineyard, rather than the rented vineyard, is far closer to what Christ was illustrating in John chapter 15:1-9.

At the conclusion of the fourteenth chapter of John, Jesus made this statement, "Get up, let us go from here". This is a good indication that chapter fifteen, and maybe all of sixteen, was a conversation on the way to the garden. If so, they could have passed quite a few small vineyards. Walking by these vineyards, Jesus might have begun to paint a mental picture for His beloved disciples, and these allegorical images were certainly created by their observation of these small family-owned vineyards.

Now the family-owned vineyard, specifically the one owned by the Bruzzo family, is cared for quite differently in many aspects when compared to the rented vineyard. In this vineyard there is only one vinedresser. As he prunes the branches, he has in mind what he is looking for as far as the end product of the fruit. The vinedresser is consumed by his vineyard, giving himself over to it, ever tending to the branches' needs, ever feeding them and ever encouraging them to grow.

This is the clearest image that we have in the Bible about the relationship between God the Father, Jesus Christ His Son and the believers in Christ.

The vinedresser knows what he wants to accomplish in the branches and the method he uses is completely different from that of the trimmers, mainly because the trimmers want quantity and the vinedresser wants quality. His goal is to produce the best wine possible, even if it means sacrificing some of the lesser quality grapes.

The wine will be produced for the vinedresser and if it is to be enjoyed by others, the works of it will bear his name on the bottles.

The end product will reflect only that of the one who cared for the branches. The trimming is done in a way that is best for the individual branches and not to cause the vineyard to have a certain appearance.

This individual trimming of each branch as a separate producer of fruit accomplishes the best overall purpose of the vinedresser. Which is for each branch to produce the best fruit that it can. No one else helps in this process because what is being established is an intimacy between the vinedresser and his branches in the vineyard.

To care for the branches in such a way is to know exactly what each one needs and this vinedresser loves the process as much as the product. Each season, the branches become stronger and more stable and produce better fruit as the relationship between the vinedresser, the vine and the branches grows.

Chapter 3

The Different Ways to
Look at a Branch

alking about the family-owned vineyard, Aldo Bruzzo makes four different types of wine. Each one of these has a completely different taste. If you were to open a bottle of La Sperugola, Merlot del Veneto 1998 and then open another bottle of the same wine only the 1999 version, although very similar, you would taste a slight difference. The reason is that man can't control the sun, the rain and the wind. These three factors are never the same from year to year, so the branches and fruit develop at different rates.

The way a branch develops determines how it should be pruned, if at all, but this is the fascinating part: there can be two vineyards side by side, with everything in common. They would have the same variety of grapes as well as the same type of soil. The sun would shine on both fields, with rain and wind identical. With all this in common, one would think that when the grapes became wine, both wines would be exactly the same. That should be true except for one missing element—the vinedresser.

If everything else was the same but the parallel fields had different vinedressers with different philosophies of pruning, everything would be different. The wines would be completely different. The method of pruning the branches determines how the fruit develops. This is the corporate, comprehensive plan of the vinedresser.

There are a number of things which are determined by the original plan of the vinedresser for the vineyard before pruning a branch. He alone knows the plan for each branch and how that fits into his overall strategy. The age of the branches, how many buds per branch, and the direction in which the branches are growing are some of the factors to look at before pruning. The plan for the branches is ultimately determined by the vinedresser.

> **"I know the plans I have**
> **For you," says The Lord**

This quotation reminds us that just as the vinedresser has a plan for each branch, so God has a plan for each of us. Isn't it fascinating how God uses something in my life that would never work for you and vice-versa?

God has a plan for all His creation. He created this world and all that is in it for a specific purpose. Although He has this comprehensive plan for all His creation, He is able nevertheless to have specific plans for the individual. Part of that plan is to bear much fruit.

**So that you will walk in a manner
worthy of the Lord,
to please Him in all respects,
bearing fruit in every good work
and increasing
in the knowledge of God;
Colossians 1:10**

God knows that you, yes you, the one reading this book, are quite different from the next person who will read it.

So God will do what is necessary for you as an individual, as far as which direction you are growing in, and how and where the pruning needs to be done. To cut out everything that does not bear fruit. God sees the plan as all about you. That's why He works. That's why He loves. That's why He sent His Son, for you.

There are many ways to look at a branch and what the branch needs determines what the vinedresser will do. In the same way, God looks at us and knows what we need. That is why He does things in my life a little differently than in yours; but His ultimate purpose is for us all to bear much fruit.

Chapter 4

Some Branches are Woven Back In

One bright spring day I was standing off in the distance watching Aldo trim a row of vines. Much like the first time I had seen this marvelous work, I observed something that made the love of the Father clearer to me. It appeared to me he would almost arbitrarily cut some branches off that were growing out into the center of the aisles. At other times, he would stretch them out and weave them back into the pattern of the rows. The work was quite slow because many of the new branches were growing this way. It's not that one branch every now and then needed this much work, but much of the vinedresser's time is spent getting the branches redirected in the path that he wants them to go. It may not be what the branch is trying to do, but then again, for the overall plan that the vinedresser is accomplishing, it is necessary. The vinedresser wants the best fruit from that branch, but he knows it can't happen in the direction it's going. He simply and lovingly redirects it, being careful not to break it.

In the same way, many believers branch off and try different ways to produce spiritual fruit. They have an idea they think will advance the Gospel only to find out that the way they have chosen doesn't always work the way they thought it would. Then God, the vinedresser, may intervene and redirect their growth.

Most of the time it is in retrospect that we see the hand of God in our lives. At times it is in the moment God intervenes that we don't understand what is happening and we can find ourselves asking God, why? God is the one who examines our lives and it is He alone who knows the purpose behind what He is doing.

If a person, a ministry, a church is heading in a direction contrary to the direction God wants them to go, that doesn't always mean that God automatically stops what they are trying to accomplish. At times He tenderly and lovingly spends His focused attention on us in order to put us back into His plan.

The vinedresser doesn't always cut a branch off.

Sometimes he moves it over to where it's next to another older branch. There are times when he will tie a young branch to one that is more mature. This provides the support it will need until it becomes strong enough to support itself. A couple of seasons later, the tie between the two can be removed because the younger branch has grown and become mature enough to support the fruit that it is producing on its own.

In the same way, our Heavenly Father knows the fruit that will one day be in our lives, so He does the same for us as the vinedresser does for his young branches. He moves us and weaves us next to that mature believer and ties us to that person or group so they may be able to help support us spiritually and to help us grow. Eventually, when we have matured enough, God takes away the tie and one day we are able to support the fruit in our lives. Who knows, you might be a branch that God will use to help support a younger one as well.

Chapter 5

Grafting in Branches

Aldo was showing me some special plants in the vineyard. They were branches that had come from different plants and had been grafted into older vines. He had taken each one of these small, helpless looking twigs, made an insertion into an already established vine, and carefully inserted the branches into the incision. He then carefully wrapped the two together with some special type of paper and bound them together with reeds. The next step was to pack around and inside the paper with sand, so as to retain moisture. He then took ice cubes and set them in the sand. As the ice melted, it would allow the branches to have more of the much-needed moisture during this delicate time. Thousands of plants were done this way and the success rate was ninety-nine percent.

You must know exactly what you are doing if you are

to have a good success rate in the grafting process. The vinedresser is constantly checking on his little branches and giving them the extra care needed for them to become established in the vine.

Looking at this marvel of nature, he began to tell me the reasoning for all this work. He said, "If you plant one of these little frail plants into the ground, it will grow and produce fruit, but the timeframe will be around four to seven years before you will be able to receive any harvest from that particular plant." He went on to say, "but if you graft new branches into the older vine that has been established years before, then the production of fruit will be the following year". So, one of the reasons is to produce fruit much earlier.

Another reason for the grafting process is for the new branches to be able to use the established root system of the very mature vine. The roots of this plant are stable and give support so that the newly grafted branches don't have to find their way through the soil to find the much-needed minerals. The only thing the branches need to do are to remain in the vine and the root system will do the rest.

You can also have different types of fruit coming from the same vine. Many branches that produce many types of grapes can grow out from the same vine. The fruit does not lose its original flavor because of the fruit it is next to. It simply continues to produce its type of grapes. This is a good lesson for the church to learn. If someone else is not producing fruit in the same way you are, as long as they are abiding in the Vine, don't worry, God knows what He is doing.

The beginning of the grafting process is how we are before knowing God; before understanding that we are all sinners and all deserve to wither and die. Then through some power that is beyond my comprehension, God sees fit, through His love, to pick us up as we struggle to survive and show us the truth of His Son. When we believe that Jesus is who He says He is, God then grafts us into Christ. He grafts us to Him because of what the Vine has already done for us while we were yet sinners. Through the crown of thorns. Through the incision in His side. Through the cross.

That baptism is, and will always be, the sustaining moisture that will keep us in the Vine and keep us from dying once we have been grafted in.

There are several types of branches that grow out from the one true Vine just like there can be several types of white grapes as well as red when harvest time arrives. I look at these as the many different denominations and ways to believe in Jesus. There are so many types of ways to view Christ and as long as He is viewed through the grace of God, as long as He is seen as the one true way and no other for salvation, then you can produce your type of fruit. But remember, Merlot is not better than Cabernet, just different. They can both become good wines; they just have a different taste. God knows exactly what He is doing by grafting in the branches. If it wasn't for the grafting process there would be only one type of grape and that can get pretty boring.

Once we are grafted in, we can produce fruit for Christ. With the Holy Spirit leading us we find ourselves in situations that give us opportunities to present the gospel in many ways. From those experiences, we have the possibility to produce fruit. We are able to draw from the depth of God in our lives. It is God that gives us our stability and our grounding. It is He that gives us the much-needed nourishment and it is He that gives us the ability to remain in His Son.

Chapter   6

Why Prune Branches that Produce Fruit?

nstead of Aldo bending a branch to cause it to grow in a certain direction, he sometimes believes it's better to cut part of the branch off. In pruning a branch that has fruit or has the potential to bear fruit the vinedresser does three things. First, he causes the branch to grow in at least two different directions. Initially the branches grow to the capacity of the existing root system. If a branch is pruned, all the energy still exists because the roots are still the same size. Because of this, that energy needs someplace to go. At least two small branches can grow out close to where the pruned branch was. If you trim a rose bush you can see this identical process in a couple of weeks.

Once the vinedresser has pruned the branch in one direction, it has the energy to grow off in other directions. It's not that the branch can't produce fruit if it grows out into the center of the aisles. The problem comes when the fruit begins to grow and it has no support from the other branches. The weight of the branch begins to pull and tear back into the other branches; the fruit dies and the wound to the other branches may cause a disease or sickness that may affect other branches. Support from the other branches is vital as the weight of the fruit gets heavier.

In the same way as believers in Christ, we must have the support of the body of Christ for the ministries we have to others. This might not appear necessary when we first start to grow and produce fruit. Sometimes it appears to us that the direction we are growing in is what God wants. After all, we are growing, but as the inevitable weight and pressures build as our ministries began to show fruit, if we grow alone long enough, damage can occur.

This is one of the strongest reasons for some type of accountability to other believers.

Next, by pruning, the vinedresser can cause the remaining fruit to be larger and healthier. By pruning a branch with fruit already on it, it effectively stops vitamins and minerals going to the discarded fruit and redirects it to the remaining grapes. Less wine is produced this way, but a far better wine.

Sometimes as Christians we spread ourselves too thin in what we think we are supposed to be doing for the cause of Christ. So we do a little of everything average, instead of a few things really well.

Don't get me wrong. We as believers should bear spiritual fruit in as many ways as we can. When God stops something we are doing for Him as abruptly as cutting off part of a branch, He often shows us that we should spend more time and energy on the areas that remain.

Lastly, the fruit-bearing branch that is pruned grows in its diameter and becomes stronger. It becomes more stable and can support more fruit the following season. It also becomes strength for the branches that grow out from it. As a branch grows in diameter it becomes less of a branch that is dependent on the others and more of one that can be depended on.

When God takes something out of our lives, sometimes painfully, it changes us and no science or theology can figure it out completely or even partially. Somehow we grow. We mature and we learn and we become more stable because of it spiritually. We are stronger children by what He does in our lives and how He does it. That makes us able to bear more fruit the next season of our lives. The more we experience with God, the more we allow Him to shape our lives, the more we become less dependent on others, the more we can be depended on.

The purpose of pruning is for the production of the fruit for God's bigger plan: that part of the grand unity which sometimes we can't see at that moment.

Pruning is normally painful. The things that God has pruned out of my life while I fought, kicking and screaming all the way, I now look back on and see the perfection in His wisdom. They are the very issues that have caused all the stability that I have.

Part Two

Summer

Growth

As the sun shines and the nourishment of rain comes and the wild wind blows, the conditions are perfect for the life of this great vineyard. The branches are feverishly growing in all directions. They reach out and hold on to anything and everything they meet. They feel they know what's best and that is to grow as far and as fast as they can. The leaves soak up the warmth of the sun as the tiny clumps of fruit began to grow. The branches begin to feel the pull of the noticeable weight of the fruit.

Chapter 7

You Can Tell How the Root System Is by What You Can See

hen looking at a grapevine, just before the harvest, you can see four specific parts to it. There is the vine itself, the branches that grow out from the vine, the leaves and the clumps of fruit. Now if you have strong branches coming out from the vine and healthy green leaves and clump after clump of beautiful, juicy grapes ready for harvest, I would say you have a healthy plant.

The part of the plant that we can't examine is the root system. It is developed, and is ever developing where no one can see it. It quietly grows and reaches deeper hour after hour, day after day and year after year. It's what gives the entire plant its stability, its strength, its health. It forges through the rock and clay in search of a cool drink of water, in search of nourishment and in search of strength for what can be seen.

The result of the foundation of the plant is those grapes we can look at: the grapes, which grow on the branches that are coming out of the vine. That's how you can tell how a root system is, by what you can see.

"But you, when you pray, go into your inner room, close the door and pray to your Father who is in secret, and your Father who sees what is done in secret will reward you" Matt.6:6

Have you ever met one of those old warriors for Christ? Those Christians you wish you could be like? The ones you read about from days gone by? The ones who inspire you to know Christ in a deeper way? I have, and his name was Leonard Ravenhill. I am a big fan of his books and devotion to our Savior. A few years ago he went home to be with The Lord, but in the early nineties, I was honored to spend some time with him and his wife Martha. Here is a man who was one of the most prolific writers on prayer and revival of his day. Not just for his time but for all time. I treasured his books like gold. He was in his mid-eighties and I in my twenties. Out of all the impressive characteristics of this man, stood one far beyond any I had seen in another living person, his prayer life. It was the very foundation of who he was. I have never known another who could pray like he did or as long as he did. The first time we prayed together I really didn't know what was going on. It was as if he stood before the throne of God in his prayers in a way that I had never known.

It was then that I had come to realize what it is that makes a man truly great. It is the foundation that only comes from an ever-developing relationship with the Creator. The fruit of your life, the health and strength of what it is that others can see, is only a byproduct of what they can't see. As we continue to spend time in prayer and devotion to God, we will forge through the rocks and clay of the soil of this life, ever establishing a greater hold on it. The stronger the foundation we have in Christ, the healthier and better our spiritual fruit is, and yes, it's easy to spot, even from a distance.

If you try to develop a relationship with God the Father only when you go to church, you will be a spiritual failure to yourself and to those around you.

The foundation and ever growing stability of a spiritual relationship with God can only come from the hours and days and years of our lives with The Creator.

Digging deeper into the endless nourishing soil of God's word and the understanding that we are nothing without Him, will inevitably cause us to have stronger and deeper roots.

When Jesus said you would know them by their fruit, He was saying by what you can see on the outside that will tell you whom their foundation is in.

C h a p t e r   8

The Drought

*D*rought: to dry up, a prolonged period of dry weather, a prolonged shortage or deficiency.

Ninety-seven degrees in the shade, and not a cloud in the sky. There is no breeze, nor the slightest sway of a tree. You can almost see the pollen in the air. If you wanted to take a shower and cool off you could, but after a few minutes your clothes would be damp again from perspiration.

It's just one of those relentless late June days in northeastern Italy. The problem is, these sweltering days have strung themselves together like pearls of fire for the past two months.

Farmers around here are no longer worried about their crops. They have resolved to start planning for the next year. The cornfields are brown and the stalks resemble parchment paper. The huge spools of hay are starting to appear in the barley fields two months before the harvest; the harvest that will not be this year.

I walked out into the vineyards and noticed the sunbleached clay with cracks in it so wide you can stick your finger in. The leaves on the branches are drooping and they appear to be a lighter shade of green than I think they should be, but at least they're not dead, not yet anyway.

I lifted up a leaf and it wouldn't even stay ridged. It lay over my hand like a dishrag. So, I walked down one of the rows wondering how much time and money it will cost to replace this whole vineyard. As I walked, I spotted some of the saplings ahead. They were planted only a few months ago and were only about the size of a pencil. Knowing how spindly they were, they had died for sure I thought as I approached. Then, I saw that they were just fine and noticed each one of them had wet soil around the base of the tiny vines. Someone had been hand watering these I thought to myself.

Then I looked up and there was Aldo coming down the row I was in with a thick tree branch on his shoulders and balancing a bucket of water tied to a rope on each end of the branch. He had been working in the fields for several days. I could tell because of the dark red sunburn that was starting to peel from his face and arms.

He squatted down and sat the two buckets gently on the ground beside me. He already knew my question and he offered the answer before I asked.

"This should be the last of them" he said, "I need to water these by hand until the drought has passed".

"But what about all these big vines that have been here for years, don't we need to water them too?" I asked in a slightly panicked voice.

"Not really, these young plants are the ones who need me right now".

I said, "Aldo I'm no expert but these older vines are dying, just look at the leaves".

His calm answer floored me. He said, "I'm sure all these plants think as you do".

Then he paused with one of those pauses when you're not sure if the person speaking is finished or not. I didn't say a word, I just waited. Looking out around the vineyard he continued his answer.

"I'm sure these plants think they are dying, but they are not, they are only suffering".

Then he looked at me and said, "in order to make the best wine, the vine has to suffer". It was as if my heart buckled under the weight of the spiritual truth in that statement. "In order to make the best wine the vine has to suffer".

After watering the last of the young vines with the two buckets, we flipped them upside down and sat on them under the shade of a tree. Aldo, the vinedresser, told me this story.

He said, "Years ago we had one of the worst droughts that I can remember. It sent many of the landowners around here into a panic and they felt they had to do something or they would lose their vines, sort of like how you are feeling now.

So, they went out and purchased or built elaborate irrigation systems for their vineyards and began watering them.

It was a short-term solution with long-term consequences. I, on the other hand, did nothing as far as irrigation even though it was a long and difficult dry spell. I have a long-term plan for my vineyard and I am willing to do what is best for the best wine.

"As you might guess, all the other land owners' vineyards looked great with big lush green leaves and the vines appeared to be as healthy as you could ever want in a vineyard. Mine struggled to survive. It was not as healthy or as aesthetically beautiful as the rest, but I knew exactly what I was doing. I spent a lot of time walking up and down these rows checking on the plants and knowing I was doing what was best. You see, the other landowners didn't want their crops to suffer, even for one season, so when the drought came they stepped in. The artificial watering allowed for a better crop than mine that year, but without a drought in a vineyard's life, it didn't need to struggle to survive. Mine really had to struggle and although it looked pretty bad as far as what you could see, something wonderful was happening that you couldn't see. In its struggle to live, the root systems had to look much harder for moisture in the soil and grew deeper and deeper looking for that moisture. The root systems of the other landowners' vineyards had to do little to survive and to this day the roots are still very shallow.

Without a deep established root system the plants need much more care. Now if even the hint of another drought comes, the landowners are far busier than I am".

"Still, that's not the main reason for my thinking. I have in my vineyard a much stronger and healthier plant because of the drought and my plants have a deeper established foundation. These plants are much healthier for going through this, which means the fruit will be much healthier. I now have a better grape and in turn I now have a better wine. I have more fruit, better fruit and a healthier plant because of the drought that I allowed to happen in the life of my vineyard. So this is why I say, 'In order to make the best wine the vine has to suffer'".

What is a drought in our lives spiritually? The word itself might not be a drought but the effects are the same.

Maybe the word drought is spelled differently for you. Maybe it is spelled loneliness or lack of direction, or a terminal illness, or divorce, or disillusionment, or whatever the word, or phrase, or feeling that fits for you in your situation this may be your drought. But the truth is, it seems like you are dying in some area of your life and to you that is drought.

God, just like the vinedresser, has a long-term plan for your life and allows droughts or tough times to come into it to make you what he wants you to be. And although it is extremely difficult at times, still it is vital that we know that He knows what He is doing.

It is the one who suffers most who
Has the most to give.

"The Son of God was made perfect through suffering"

"The church historically has grown the most
When it has been under persecution"
-Otis Brady-

Chapter 9

Branches Need Time to
Produce Quality Fruit

When a grapevine is planted, the vinedresser does not expect the branch to produce fruit the first few years. The plant is only required to grow and mature. It needs time to become established in the soil and as each season passes it becomes more stable. Eventually, the fruit-producing years of the branches will begin. The first year's fruit will be fairly sparse as the plant slowly continues to grow deeper down into the soil looking for more minerals to draw from. All the grapes from that first year's production will be harvested and added in with the older branches' fruit even though the amount of the individual production is rather scarce. Each year the branches become stronger as the roots dig deeper and farther looking for the much-needed food that is provided by the minerals in the soil. As the seasons pass, with each new harvest the quality of the grapes continues to increase. The quantity of the fruit increases as well as the quality. The grapes become more potent with a higher sugar content and thus they become better fruit.

The vinedresser knows that the branches, at about the ten-year point of the fruit producing years, will reach the point where they are as strong as they're going to be. Now the branches can be relied on. The vinedresser knows what to expect as far as the quality of the fruit from those branches. This is what he intended from the beginning.

During these early years of the branch's life, the vinedresser patiently waits. He doesn't think about the potential, that one day they will produce fruit for the harvest, he sees grapevines. He sees them for what they already are. The branches won't become branches, they are branches. They won't produce anything for a while, and that's just fine for the vinedresser, they will just work on growing for now.

I was nineteen years young and ready to change the world for Christ. I had just dedicated my life to my newfound Savior and I was busy about the Father's business, or so I thought. I was one of those early eighties crowd that was swept into the Kingdom through the ministry of Keith Green[1]. To use a cliché that has been beaten to death, I was on-fire for Christ. I think now in retrospect, I made more mistakes than progress. My zeal ablaze for Christ was more of an anxious flame-thrower burning people at the stake. In my witnessing with an attitude, I would turn on one person for Jesus and turn off two. Then I would turn off two more people and turn on one. I figured that two for six wasn't bad and that must just be the way God does math. At the time it never occurred to me that I might not be doing things right.

I didn't miss a youth retreat, as they were called then, from any church that invited me. The first year of my new birth I went on thirteen week-end excursions to get closer to God. I don't know if I did get closer to the Lord during those weekends but I sure sang Kum Ba Yah a lot by the campfire. I could quote most all of the words to the popular Christian contemporary songs, but I couldn't quote hardly anything from the word of God.

I have fond memories of the first few years of being born into the kingdom of God, but now I see how slow

---

[1]Keith Green was a Christian contemporary musician, singer and song-writer who God used to bring much of a nation back to Himself and the affects of his love and music are being felt at this very hour. He died on July 28th 1982.

I really grew back then. I didn't grow spiritually because I chose not to. I have come to believe through experience that it is the grace of God that sustains us. There is a time in the early years of attempting to serve God that He wants us to just get to know Him. To learn about Him through His word and by what is around us.

To know about Christ is to know there is water on a hot summer's day, to know Christ is to drink of that water.

There was fruit produced in those early years but not a lot. With each passing year of trying to produce spiritual fruit when I should have been using my energies to grow in the vine of Christ, I did very little. Still, whatever fruit there is gets harvested together with all the other fruit of that crop.

God knows all this about us before our parents get to see us for the first time. He doesn't see future potential. He doesn't see us as children who will one day advance His kingdom. He doesn't see us for what we will one day become. He sees His children. He sees who and what we already are, joint heirs with His Son Jesus Christ. God is quite happy spending His time with us and longs for us to spend it all with Him. He is not concerned about the fruit we will produce at all compared to the time He wants us to spend getting to know Him. If we first draw near to God, He will draw near to us and because of this we will produce fruit.

Remember, spiritual fruit is a by-product or a result of abiding in The Vine.

John 15:8
By this is My
Father glorified,
that you bear
much fruit,
and so prove to be
My disciples

Chapter 10

The Vine is Everything To the Branches

"Abide in Me and I in you. As the branch cannot bear fruit of itself unless it abides in the vine, so neither can you unless you abide in Me".
John 15:4

A branch is not a branch at all if it is not growing. It's only a dry stick or splintery twig. If a branch is growing, that does not mean it is merely attached to a vine, but rather it is living from within a vine and the vine itself is inside the branch.

The vine is the life for the branch and must do absolutely everything for it. Because the vine lives, it is able to draw the much-needed vitamins and minerals from the rich soil of the earth and pass it along to the branches. It is the vine that enables the branches to continue to grow. The branches apart from the vine have no life. They are only dead brush that can be gathered together and one strike of fire, a puff of smoke, and they are nothing at all.

Without the branch abiding or remaining in the vine, it can do nothing at all; it can't even live. If we do not abide or remain in Christ, we can do nothing at all; we can't live spiritually. We think of our technological advancements and how far we've come in such a relatively short period of time and we feel we can do anything. What obstacles can stop us? What problem is there that we can't overcome given a little time? Even nature can no longer hide from us. We have unraveled the secret mysteries of DNA. If there is something elusive to us, we will track it down. We are in charge, and as a society, we no longer need the vine. A savior? Who could possibly need a savior today? What do we need to be saved from anyway, asks the most profane generation since the birth of Jesus.

Our prayers have become something we tack on after a long day and before we have a meal. When we have time and if it fits into our schedule, we will abide in Christ. I'll stop here and save this for another book. It'll suffice for now to say it is still possible to have some works, but they will be burned up in the fire and be only a pile of ashes without abiding in Christ.

I have found myself in the past trying to do rather than just being.

When I had a younger man's skin, I found myself doing as much "Christian stuff" as I could. I was going on every youth retreat available and going to any and all special meetings the church had to offer. I visited the hospitalized and homeless. Prayer meetings, I was there. Of course I made it to the Wednesday night Bible study, Sunday School, morning church, and evening church. I even passed out tracts in the front of rock concerts with some friends until one of my team told a guy coming out of the concert that Jesus loved him. We spent the next few hours in the emergency room getting his broken nose fixed. We didn't know there was danger involved in serving Christ so we changed to a much safer telephone ministry.

I quickly got to the point where I thought God needed me to do all this Christianizing or it just wasn't going to get done. Reading my Bible became something I did when I found the time and back then I just couldn't find any. I had no idea what was happening, but I was trying to be so busy doing the things I thought Christians should do that my personal relationship with my Savior became just a casual acquaintance.

This is a good time for disaster to come into your life as suddenly as a tsunami, and of course it did. I wasn't doing anything for the cause of Christ I was being busy for the cause of Robert Scott Stiner.

God doesn't love us because of what we can do for Him, He loves us because of who we are. If we try to show God how much we love Him by what we do for Him, we will only feel we have to earn His love. Christ put an order to the work process of the Kingdom. He said abide in Me, and I will abide in you. Get to know who I am, what I stand for, how much I love you. Understand your identity in Me and after this happens you will bear fruit as a result of our relationship.

I found that I couldn't do anything accurately without Christ. He has to do everything for me because without Him I dry up like a branch with no nourishment. The vine is everything to the branches and Christ is everything to us. He loves being everything to us.

Chapter 11

As the Branches Gets Older
The Roots Go Deeper

ave you ever read a passage in the Bible and it had a
specific meaning to you? A meaning that meant little
to others, but it meant everything to you the first time
you noticed it? A verse that gave some type of direction
for one of the many paths God has sent you down?
Maybe much needed help or comfort from a part of the
Bible has taken away the sting in a moment of loss or
crisis? Has direction been shown to you through the
Word of God in a verse that spoke to your very soul? I
think we all have experienced this to some degree. We
go along in life and treasure the jewel of those words in
our hearts, don't we?

Later in life we find ourselves reading over the same
passage in the scriptures, but sometimes we see it
differently from the time before. It almost jumped off

the page and burrowed into your heart and mind in a way that makes us say: "I have never noticed that in that way before!"

You read the word of God all the time. Your Bible is dog-eared and the pages you have highlighted so much they look like an abstract work of art. Some sections you almost know by heart, but you still read them over again. Then it seems as if part of the page grows into a font ten times larger than the rest of the page and you just stare at it. You read it again and again and you see something in a completely different way than you ever thought of before. That same verse that meant one thing a few years ago now means something far deeper to you.

What has changed? Not God's word, it never changes. It is you and I who change, and we are ever changing, ever growing, ever maturing.

As we travel through this life, the experiences that we encounter and how we deal with those experiences shape us and change the lenses which we see through. Our paradigm changes as we grow, so we are able to see another layer in the depth of God's word.

As we get older, our relationship with our Lord Jesus Christ grows deeper. Sometimes we think back to just a few years before and say to ourselves that we can't believe the choices we made then.

The more we learn about our Savior and the more we spend time with Him, the wiser we become.

Chapter 12

The Vinedresser Uses Different Techniques in Training His Branches

ome branches grow wildly out into the center of the aisles. Some get wrapped around each other and a few follow the pattern of the branches from the previous year.

As the vinedresser looks at the individual branches, He sees that they don't all grow the same way. Because of this, they must be pruned in the way that is best for the individual branch to produce the most amount of fruit. At the same time, they must also be pruned in the way that fits the overall plan of the vinedresser.

Our heavenly Father sees us as individuals and does for our lives what is best for us as individuals, as well as fitting us into the comprehensive plan He is accomplishing.

I have a friend who can read something in the Bible and apply what he has read to his life. From that moment on, he is forever changed for the better. I, on the other hand, am not so easily taught. There have been things that God has had to show me over and over again. There have been lessons from God that I have had to learn and that have soaked into my way of life at about the same speed a drop of water can soak into a slab of granite.

We end up in the same place eventually, but because my friend is submissive to the will of God while I can fall a little on the rebellious side, I end up with the bruises of life that he didn't have to endure.

God has always known our individual shortcomings. Mine are probably a little different from yours, so the way He trains us at times may be a little different. His overall plan for His finished product however, is the same.

I've watched Aldo take two branches intertwined and growing together and ever so gently untangle them. If he didn't do this, once the fruit started growing it wouldn't develop properly. The fruit would compete for the same space and at that point, Aldo would not be able to separate the branches from each other and would have no alternative but to trim the branches and the fruit would be lost.

He can see the result of letting branches grow around each other. Even though the problems won't arise until the end of the season, he can foresee what is coming in the near future.

So he lovingly untangles the branches so they can both produce fruit in the proper time. On the other hand, the branches themselves will rarely understand what is happening to them. The branches that grow intertwined like this are for a while able to support themselves and can't see the problems that will arise once the weight of the fruit begins.

Eventually the branch can understand the loving hand of the vinedresser, but for the most part only after the branches have been untangled. Of course, that is if a branch could think like you and I.

There are many branches just like there are many members in the body of Christ.
As a vineyard produces fruit corporately, each

individual branch produces fruit as well. For without the individual branches, there is no production.

As the body of Christ, we must produce fruit as individuals and this makes up the corporate production of fruit for God. The fruit that I produce in my life may not be the exact fruit that you produce. The needs that people have are so varied. The type of need that one person might have that you are near, may be quite different from the person with the need that I may be near. So God, in His infinite wisdom, shapes our lives in different ways and it is always in ways to where we can meet the needs of those around us and produce the best fruit, the most fruit for Him. This is one of the reasons He prunes us all a little different.

Another reason is that we do not all produce the same amount of spiritual fruit. God prunes us in ways that we will produce the amount of fruit for His purpose and that might be more or less that the next person. One of the Christians biggest hang-ups is that we see our brother or sister doing what we consider to be a great work of God and we compare our production of fruit to theirs. If I measured what I do against what Charles Swindoll does it could throw me into a pit of despair. Remember, it is not about us, it's about Jesus.

Chapter 13

"The Vinedresser Isn't in a Hurry"

$\mathcal{J}$ think the first thing I learned fairly well was to work on automobiles. I never thought I'd do it for a living, but I did enjoy it. Having a small landscaping company would follow. Drawing the designs, then building projects and installing the plants until the plan had reached fruition, was a lot of fun. That would end one day and I would be off to the next idea. Stained glass lamps and windows would be another passion of mine and after that, something else. Wiring a house, fixing a VCR, putting a roof on, playing music, it seems like it has never ended with me. You may be thinking that you know someone just like that. Or then again, maybe my story reminds you of you. Well, eventually I would become a missionary in Central America. Guess which one of those skills I would use as I worked in my new life? What do you think it is that God would use in me from my pre-missionary days? Everything! All the abilities and experience I had would play a vital role in what God's plan was for the mission field. For example, Otis Brady and myself were coming back from dropping off some building supplies for a church. In a torrential downpour, the tie-rod on the front wheel of our truck broke. This caused the tire to lean into the truck rendering the vehicle unmovable. So on the clay dirt roads that quickly turned to mud, I worked on the tie-rod. In 30 minutes or so, I fixed it to the point where we could get back to town. Later, I would lead a team in wiring one of our new churches in a village that would soon be having electricity. Teaching the villagers how to make glass projects was an unbelievable way of sharing my faith.

My point is this; there are lessons that God wants to teach us that are not always immediate and the timetable is up to God, not us, on when we are going to be used for His purposes. Some jobs, experiences and even people come into our lives and we hope it will never end. But, being a missionary, I have seen that timing is everything; not my timing but God's. He is a patient God and He is a loving God and the time He needs to take specifically for you He will joyfully take. When He looks at you, He knows there are no other branches exactly like you. He already knows about the harvest that will come from your life and He knows the time it will take before you are ready. Sometimes it might be a while off. Remember that Moses was forty years in preparation before there would be a harvest from his life. The apostle Paul would spend most of his life before any good fruit was produced. Sometimes in our own lives we can't see a thing and we bounce around from one thing to the next. So, when looking at a person remember that the vinedresser spends the time necessary for each of his branches in order to have His fruit produced in the proper time.

Chapter 14

Some Branches Grow Correctly

*E*very now and then while Aldo is working through the vineyard, he will come to a branch that needs very little if anything at all done to it. This is a branch that from the vine has grown in the proper direction as well as the correct size and vigor for the fruit it will produce. When coming upon one of these rare branches, the vinedresser can only smile as his plans for the production of fruit are the same as those of the branch, without making changes to it.

Otis and Martha Brady are the best examples of this phenomenon that I have. You would be hard-pressed to find better ones anywhere. Thirty-eight years they spent as missionaries in countries other than their own. They raised three amazing children and countless believers. Otis and Martha built churches, raised up pastors, led worship, housed the homeless and fed the hungry.

Leonard Ravenhill wrote me a letter while I was in Belize and it simply said, "there are those who point the way to Christ and there are those who lead the way to Christ". The Bradys have led the way to Christ by taking me, and so many others, by the hand and showing us Christ.

For the better part of a year, I lived with Otis and Martha, in that country of contrasts and because of them I have come to know this. It's very rare, but there are a few who grow exactly where God wants them to grow, all their lives. I don't know how many times I stepped over the homeless who were sleeping in the living room to get to my room. Martha always made room for the person who stopped by to say hello conveniently around lunchtime.

The Bradys are perfect examples of a branch that rarely if ever needs pruned. A couple who has given the best years of their lives for the cause of Christ.

Part Three

Autumn

Harvest

*It's late September and the hue of light is almost ready
to announce the breaking of a new day,*

*like a symphony the moment before
the conductor looks up*

and the music of the light of day bursts into song.

*The warm wind begins to blow
and the sun illuminates the dew
on the leaves;*

*in waves the vineyard dances.
The day is perfect and so is the fruit of the vine.*

*The branches hold as tightly to their prize as
God holds to His children.*

Chapter 15

*Preparation for
The Harvest*

In My Father's house are many rooms...

here's a lot to do around the Bruzzo's before the harvest begins. The hand pruners for all the laborers must be inspected and oiled. The wine press must be cleaned. Fixing the tractor and the machines takes time if something isn't working properly. Basically, getting everything ready takes a couple of weeks, but the two most important items on the list are to prepare the cantina and to go through the vineyards one last time and clean the branches.

The Bruzzo's villa is as romantic as you'll ever see. It has a terra-cotta multi-leveled tile roof with big arched doorways and rounded weathered doors. Geraniums are in the window boxes and several animals are usually in the driveway. The big white stucco villa overlooks the vast expanse of their rolling vineyards that surround the home. And the pyramid stack of wine barrels along with the picnic tables are under an oak tree that have witnessed at least seventy summers as it reaches out in all directions. And the outdoor pizza oven that the locals used to come over on Sundays and bake bread still works great.

One of the great aspects about it is where the wine is kept. The cantina is part of the house. You simply go through a doorway from the kitchen and you are looking at rows of oak wine barrels where part of the wine is kept. Continuing through another entrance you are surrounded by huge vats of ever-curing wine which will one day be bottled with the name of Ca'Bruzzo on them. It takes a lot of work to prepare such an area and Aldo and his son work together preparing to bring the fruit of their labor into their home. This must be completed before the harvest so all the fruit can be brought into their villa. Timing is everything when it comes to the vinedresser.

The Shitre Erusin

In ancient times the Jewish people had very specific wedding ceremonies. Before the wedding there was the betrothal. The betrothal period was a time of engagement for the couple to be wed. It basically went like this for the Galilean region. If a man found a woman he would like to make his wife, he would make the request to her in a formal way with a letter or offer an amount of money. If she agreed, a betrothal ceremony would be arranged. This was a small intimate gathering with an officer of the church to perform the ceremony, a couple of witnesses and the couple to be betrothed. At this ceremony, the man and woman would offer their dowries and the bridegroom would have the betrothal contract called the *Shitre Erusin* drawn up. This contract would state several points from the husband to the bride to be. After both parties had signed it, it would be so binding that it would be the same as if the couple were already married, with the exception of living together and consummating the marriage. In fact, after the Shitre Erusin was completed and signed by the two to be wedded, the witnesses and the overseeing officer, it would take a written letter of divorce to break the contract. If the future husband died, the woman would still receive the inheritance that was stated in the contract as well. In this binding contract, one of the points stated would say that the man would supply the place to live for himself and his bride after the wedding. The time it would approximately take for the man to build the home for them to live in was listed as well. The building would happen like this, after the contract was completed the bride-to-be would go back to her parent's home and the groom would go back to his parent's home. The son and his father would build on another living area for his bride and himself to live in. The groom's father's house is where the newly married couple would live. After the wedding, the new husband would take his bride to his father's house where the new rooms had been built.

This was as common a practice as the drinking of wine to those simple, earnest, honest people who lived in the hills of Galilee.

Jesus spoke these words to His disciples in His farewell discourse to them.

"In My Father's house are many dwelling places;
if it were not so I would have told you;

for I go to prepare a place for you".
"If I go and prepare a place for you, I will come
again and receive you unto Myself, that where I am,
there you may also be".
John 14:2-3

There it is. Jesus spoke the 'Shitre Erusin' to His disciples and they knew exactly what he meant when He did. He said to His disciples and also to us today, that we, as the bride of Christ, are betrothed to Christ. Christ said that there were many places in His Father's house and that He was leaving now to go and prepare the places for us. He also said that when the rooms were complete and the time was right, He was coming back for us because we are His precious bride. (My paraphrase)

We have our contract; our document that is signed and witnessed called the Holy Bible and it is the best contract ever written. It tells us how much we are loved. It tells us of our inheritance. It tells us that we are not forgotten and we are of extreme value and that Christ is coming back for us.

God the Father witnessed it as it was being written

and it was signed and sealed by Jesus Christ. He made sure everyone knew it was His signature because He signed it with His blood.

I'll bet the time from the Betrothal to the wedding seemed to go far too slow for the bride. To see her husband and spend the rest of her life with him was something she wanted and longed for. I know that it's slow for me waiting for Christ to return.

For now I'll be more than content to wait and produce fruit.

Jesus is preparing a home for me and if you believe He is who He says He is, then Jesus is preparing a home for you as well. I don't know of any more comforting words in all of scripture than these; to know that Christ is coming back for His bride.

Chapter 16

One Last Trip Through
The Vineyards

Aldo makes one last trip through his vineyards in preparation for the harvest. This is called cleaning the branches. He is looking for anything he can do one last time for them before the workers come through. Cleaning the branches consists of many things. Sometimes it is to take off some of the big leaves that might be shading the clumps of grapes. This is for two reasons, first if the grapes are partially covered with leaves then it takes longer to dry out the clusters of fruit with the warmth of the sun. Grapes must be completely dry on the outside before they can be picked. Moisture turns into mildew, which can destroy the entire harvest.

The second reason the vinedresser takes off some of the leaves is to make the fruit more visible to the workers. If this isn't done, the harvesters may miss the fruit and it will probably die on the vine. It's a very sad thing for me to walk through a vineyard in the late fall, when the leaves have fallen off the branches, and see fruit that has been left behind.

"For God so loved the world, that He gave His only begotten Son, that whoever believes in Him shall not perish, but have eternal life".

John 3:16

To believe the words that Jesus Christ spoke. That He is the One He says He is, is to be clean.

Chapter 17

Gathering the Workers

And He was saying to them,
"The harvest is plentiful, but the laborers are few;
therefore beseech the Lord of the harvest to
send out laborers into His harvest".

Luke 10:2

$\mathcal{T}$he harvest is only a week away as Aldo starts making
the calls to all the friends and family that will be a part
of this amazing experience. You can hear the
excitement in his voice as he speaks to one of his many
relatives on the phone that everything is just about
ready. He couldn't possibly bring the harvest in by
himself and so many others will come to help. Without
the workers, the fruit would eventually began to rot or
deteriorate on the branches, so the vinedresser needs to
have workers standing by ready to work when he says
the time has come. Only a few are not going to be able

to help this year but many other new friends have decided to help out, so everything has worked out perfectly.

Standing by the window and with curiosity, I watch the silhouettes of Italians walking up the drive as the early morning begins to break. Some are riding their bicycles with the wicker baskets mounted on the front handlebars. As they filter in, I see they all have on the attire of laborers. The ladies have on wide-brimmed hats to keep the sun off and the kind of short sleeved shirts and pants you would wear if you knew that at the end of the day you would be covered in permanent fruit-stains. Everyone has on comfortable-looking shoes. They know they will be standing and walking most of the day.

Aldo is there to greet them and the mood is almost festive rather than that of work. He opens his arms wide as he gives a big embrace to a relative and a kiss on both cheeks. For the workers, it is a joyous time to know that all the passion and love of the vinedresser has come to fruition and now they will take part in the process as they prepare to bring in the fruit from the season.

God has called us to work. He has said to the believers of this generation that we are a part of the work for His kingdom.

Throughout all of history, the world we live in has never needed guidance and direction any more than it does right now. Never has there been another time when so many supposed answers have titillated our intellect and given us options on how to achieve spiritual fulfillment. The world as a whole and as individuals, are longing for truth, for answers, real answers and there are none without Christ.

This is the field. The field of human hurt and the void of the human soul. The answer I'm sure is in the saving grace of Jesus Christ and that great mandate to the seventy in Luke chapter ten applies to us today, at this very moment. We are told that there is a harvest that is ready and a harvest to be had by those who are willing to work for the Lord of that harvest.

What a great gift to be given. The opportunity of being a part of bringing in a harvest in which the Vinedresser has already done the work.

No wonder Aldo's friends and family are in a festive mood as I watch them being gathered together even though there is work to be done.

The Best Wine Comes from the Fruit Closest to the Vine

But now faith,
hope, and
love,
abide these three;
But the greatest
of these is
love.

1 Corinthians 13:13

hen it comes to making the best wine, there are certain things a vinedresser understands. One of those things is using the best grapes. These are the grapes that are the healthiest, the most potent, and the ones with the most vitamins and minerals received from the soil. Let's call these the best fruit.

The best fruit are the clusters of grapes that are closest to the vine.

If I took one branch and stretched it out in a straight line starting from the vine to the tip of the other end, this is what we would notice.

The first clump of grapes closest to the vine would be the largest and the most potent, receiving the best of the vine's nutrition.

The second clump closest to the vine would be the next largest and second only to the first clump as far as potency goes, and so on down the line. The farther you get away from the vine the more the potency, size and health of the fruit diminishes. Being close to the vine has its benefits.

Aldo told me that "the first three clumps of grapes closest to the vine are the best to use if you want to make the best wine possible".

The rest of the grapes don't have anything wrong with them and can still be harvested to make good wine. However, here I am only speaking of the most sought after fruit; the fruit that can do the most good; the fruit that the vinedresser seeks for his overall plan and purpose, if he is to make the best wine.

The Apostle Paul in 1 Corinthians chapter thirteen speaks of this very thing spiritually in verse thirteen.

But now faith, hope, love, abide these three; but the greatest of these is love.

Out of all the virtues one can have there are but three that are the strongest, the healthiest, and the closest to the vine. These three are the most sought after and needed by God. God seeks your faith. God seeks your hope in Him. God wants your love.

The most sought after fruit, the number one fruit to produce by a believer in Jesus Christ should be love.

Love is the strongest force in every universe that has ever been and ever shall be.
Love is the reason God gave us His Son as a gift to you and to me.
It's the reason this world on its axis continues to spin. The reason we continue to breathe in spite of our sin.
Love is the reason Jesus said I must go but I'll never leave you, NEVER.

Love is the reason He is preparing a place to live in forever.

Love is the reason He said that when it is finished He would come back and take us there.

If I were to define love in a word, it would be the Galilean I'm writing about. That word would be the name Jesus! If you desire to pursue real love then you desire Christ. So, there is no question about what the greatest fruit should be in our lives.

As a branch, if we abide in The Vine the first fruit is love. The love that Christ has for us and the love that we have for Him and the love that we must have for each other is the best fruit we can produce.

Chapter 19

The Quality of the Wine Depends on...

here are many factors that determine the quality of a
wine. The wind, rain and sun are very important, as
we have seen in a previous chapter. To achieve the best
quality in a wine, one must pay far more attention to the
grapes being used. A good quality wine can very
quickly be brought down to just an average table wine
by one thing, bad grapes. A few rotting or molded
grapes on a clusters if not picked from it, can lessen the
integrity of a whole crate of fruit. Rot or mold travels
very quickly through the rest of the fruit it comes in
contact with, and the result, if not detected early, can be
devastating to the quality of the wine. You will still end
up with wine, but these bad grapes could very well end
up being the difference between an average wine and a
high quality wine.

The church was thriving. It was really something to see how one church could have such a positive impact on a community. There were canned food drives for the needy when there wasn't a holiday in sight. There were door-to-door visits by members of the church as they went around helping the elderly with some of the chores that had become too burdensome for them. It was quite common to see one of the three vans with their name on the side of it, pull up to a house and two or three people get out and start cutting the grass or raking the leaves for someone who needed help. The members shared the gospel through what they did as well as what they said. The non-believers in Christ had to sit up and notice that this church was different from what they had been led to believe about Christians and it was working, people started coming to this church because of what they were seeing. The pastor of the church was the brainchild behind this outburst of spiritual fruit to the community and everyone loved him for his efforts in attempting to draw their community to Christ. The church was growing like never before because of one man's plan to win his community to Christ and the congregation's efforts.

Until.

You knew there was an until, didn't you?

Until the news got out about the pastor and another woman in the congregation, other than his wife. This is the kind of news that travels through a community like a Florida brush fire on a windy day. Nothing can stop it. You put up barriers and it jumps them. The pastor of the church was asked to resign and the congregation was devastated and stunned both at the same time. Disillusionment has a way of forcing its way into the minds of people in times of crisis.

The assistant pastor took over as head of the church and did very well in getting the church through that time of crisis. He also continued the same outreach to the community in the same way as the pastor before him, but the results were very different. The church didn't grow much after that. As a matter of fact, the church got about thirty percent smaller than before. The congregation's bombardment of questions and I-told-you-so's from the community of non-believers in Christ made their work much harder. They still ministered to the town through their work, but for a season the potency of their spiritual fruit was extremely diminished.

Chapter 2 0

Bringing in the Harvest

*I*t's a perfect morning for the harvest. The sun is coming up and with a whisper of a breeze the workers are filtering out into the vineyard. It's a sight to see, this harvesting by hand of one man's work. Aldo has given instructions on which rows to work in and what to look for. The workers are all in the rows working their way to the other end cutting the clumps of fruit off the branches and putting them into crates that are strewn throughout the fields. Many are singing and laughing while the work is being accomplished as they carefully look so as not to miss any fruit. It feels like this is more of a party than that of labor, and in a way it is. The year-long work that the vinedresser has done is the most laborious and detailed and Aldo and his son are right in the midst of it all. They are cutting off the fruit and singing just like the next person.

The crates fill up quickly and other people pick them up after they have become heavy with the fruit and walk the crates to the end of the rows where they are being stacked.

Christ has called us to walk out into the ripe harvest of this world which is lost without Him. We are all needed to bring in this harvest of souls to the kingdom. The time is perfect. The temperature is perfect. So come join this harvest. There are already some workers out in the fields now but Christ needs you to help. The instructions have already been given and you know what to do, so come on and give a hand.

Part Four

Winter

Rest

After the harvest has come and gone and the vines have given up their fruit, after the leaves have turned from a lush green to pale yellow to brown and fallen to earth and blown away, we see the lonely, barren vineyard again. Row after row over the rolling hills and into the valleys in all directions are the grapevines with the branches that had grown wildly throughout the season. Now they are at rest. It seems to be a time of reflecting on the past harvest when the workers were in the fields gathering the fruit. It was hard and exhausting work, but it was exciting and a joyful time as we brought in the harvest that would be turned into new wine and shared by all.

There is a man walking down the path to the vineyards. He walks around the perimeter of the field and stands at a point where he can see the entire expanse of his work. The man appears to have many years behind him as shown by the lines in his face and the silver in his hair. His attire is that of a laborer with warm clothes and work boots. It looks like he is going to be in the fields for a long time. The man has two items with him, a bag of something, and hand pruners for cutting small branches.

Chapter 21

The Vinedresser is Always in the Field

Aldo is always working in his vineyard. It's not an issue of spending a few hours each week in the fields, but rather nearly all of his time is spent in the pursuit of stronger and healthier branches.

There are several prunings per year, not just one, and these take a large portion of his time. He seems always to be mending fences, tying up branches that have fallen, re-staking plants and checking on his beloved vineyard.

You can't get him to take a vacation and you can barely get him to leave the property. He is doing what he loves to do in his own fields. To Aldo, taking care of the vineyard is a vacation. You can say or try anything you want, but the vinedresser just isn't leaving the fields. It can be the foggiest day in Italy and visibility can be two feet in front of you, and he will be somewhere out there in the midst of it all, working.

It can be pouring down rain, blistering hot or freezing cold and the vinedresser is right in the middle of the lives of his branches.

Checking, always checking, always helping, always supporting. Doing what is best for those branches even if the branches don't feel it would be the best thing to do.

I think it gives us a little more insight about how God feels towards us. He doesn't come into our lives a few hours per week and the rest of the time we're on our own. He is always there. Whether we feel him there or not He is there. Whether we see Him or not, He is always there. God is doing that which He loves to do, taking care of His prize possessions, His children. When He said He'd never leave you and never forsake you He meant it. He meant it two thousand years ago and He means it at this very moment. It can be the foggiest period in your life that you have ever known, spiritually. It can be so bad that you can't see the next step or which way to turn, but you can at least know this, God is not on vacation. He is with His prize possessions, as a matter of fact; He is standing right beside you.

You can be in the downpour of depression. You can be in the blistering furnace of false accusations or even beside the freezing cold door of the death of a loved one and you can still know that there is no other place our Heavenly Father desires to be than right beside you. God wants you to be strong and God wants you to be healthy spiritually. That's why He is always checking, always wanting to help and He is and always will be your biggest fan.

Chapter 22

"Replacing Those Supports"

Have you ever noticed that just when things get comfortable, just when we start to like the way things are, God forces us from the comfort that we have grown accustomed to?

Once a season, normally in the winter, the vinedresser goes through the vineyards and cuts off the old bands of support that were put on last year and replaces them with new ones. After only one season they loose their elasticity. They no longer stretch as the plant grows, but instead the bands become ridged. This rigidity can bind or choke out the growth and expansion of the plant and cause harm instead of helping to support it. The new bands expand with the growth of the branch and this gives the plants the ability to be supported as they continue growing.

I have a good friend whom I will call James. He's a missionary and he and his family lived in Europe up until a year ago, where they had served for no less than ten years with a missions organization. It is impossible to count the number of lives James touched. Impossible to calculate the number of truths bestowed upon those who gleaned from his teachings and example. Impossible to claim to know how much James loved his work. I remember setting and listening to him teach and thinking how much God loved me to allow me to hear this man speak and change my heart. At one point, he could see himself being a part of this ministry for as long as he was alive on this earth. The support of a mission board, supporters, friends and family for ten years was firmly in place. No other had lasted as long in this line of work, in this area of the world as James had or probably ever will again. He and his family spoke the language and truly loved the country. His children were being raised there and in the local school system. However, in the course of about a year it was all over. James and his family were back in the States. It was as if God had cut off that which he had grown to love; that which had supported him; that which he had become accustomed to.

But, just like Aldo the vinedresser that I watch in the

field, when he cuts off that support, his hand is already firmly in place to hold that which he loves,while he puts the new support around the plant for the next season.

God had indeed cut off that support in James' life because if it had continued any longer, that old support, just like on the plant, would have begun to cause harm to the process instead of help. God holds us in His hands and it is His grace that holds us and will not allow us to break off from the vine and fall to the ground.

I have found myself in similar situations to those experienced by my friend James. With the exception that I have seen God coming with those pruners in His hand. I have in the past become quite comfortable with my surroundings. I was enjoying where I had been and what I had been doing. I had not yet learned the spiritual truth that, with comfort comes the baggage of complacency.

So, the next time we begin to ask why about something in our lives, and feel that God has walked away from us, and feel that He is giving us more than we can bear, say these words: His grace holds us. Allow these simple words to be the rising tide in your spirit until it floods your soul:

His grace holds us.

Never forget this!

Chapter 23

His Name is on the Bottles

"A good name is to be more desired
than great riches".

Proverbs 22:1a

When you see a bottle of wine from Aldo's vineyard and when looking at the label, you will notice the name on it reads Ca'Bruzzo which is the name of their winery standing for Casa di Bruzzo, or House of Bruzzo's. Bruzzo is Aldo's last name which you may already know by now. His name being on the bottle has a different meaning from many other wines in the region, though they may have their names on their bottles as well. Aldo is the only vinedresser in his vineyard and the others may well have many trimmers as we have discussed in previous chapters, but this one man's passion and heart and soul have gone into taking care of his branches. I have seen it as a relationship where he has taken the best of care of the branches and in return they have produced the best possible fruit as individual branches, given their individual size and vigor.

So in essence, when you see that bottle of wine, you will know that part of the vinedresser is in that bottle. That red wine is like his signature. It is his name. It is who he is.

Some people have jobs they love doing, others do jobs where their love is the result of what they do. This would be the vinedresser.

If a below average wine was produced, it might speak volumes about the winery. In the same way, if an outstanding wine is produced, it also can speak volumes about that winery.

We are the body of Christ. We, as believers in Jesus, make up the branches that God, the Vinedresser, works through to produce spiritual fruit to a sick, disillusioned and dying world. The more we abide in Christ, the more we are one with the Father. The more we learn to follow the leading of the Holy Spirit, the better fruit will be produced for His kingdom.

It is the name of Christ that is with the believers in Him. It is the love of God that has been poured into us. It is His heart and passion and soul that is turned toward us and has gone into our lives. God tenderly and caringly spends the necessary time with us and does for us what needs to be done, so His overall plan is accomplished in our lives.

It is the signature of God that has been clearly marked on the souls of those belonging to Him. So in a way you could say that His name is on those who believe in His son. We are the ones with the name, House of God, put on us and with the new wine poured into our lives.

Chapter 24

A Healthy Plant can't help but Produce Fruit

One of the meanings of the word abide is to hold on. That is all we are required to do, just hold on. Just stay abiding in Christ and He will abide in us. As the Vinedresser prunes us, we can't help but produce fruit. Producing fruit is a byproduct of holding onto Jesus. The work has already been done.

So holding on is all we can do. We can't produce fruit for the Kingdom of God without Christ. Many have tried and all have failed.

There are whole religions that are based on working for a reward. If we try to produce good works in our lives to show God how much we love Him then our relationship becomes conditional. But if we have a healthy and accurate understanding of abiding in Christ first, the good works that we were created for will surface.

If we as believers can grasp this truth, it will make producing fruit much easier.

To understand our place in the Kingdom of God, to understand that we are joint heirs with Jesus Christ and that we are loved without having to do or become anything, brings a sense of joy that you must experience to believe or understand. This truth compels us to desire to pass this gift on to others so they may have what we have. So just hold on, just remain, just abide and you will bear fruit.

Jesus said in John 14:6 "I am the way, and the truth, and the life; no one comes to the Father but through Me".

Through Me.

Through Me.

Through Me.

Chapter 25

A Season of Rest

J n the life of a vineyard, it is necessary for it to have a period of resting or lying dormant. It's one of those conditions that is very necessary, but most frequently forgotten. The vineyard appears to be dead, but it is very much alive in spite of its appearance. The leaves have fallen to the ground and returned to the dust from where they had come. The fruit is gone. All the green on the plant and all outward showings of life are gone. The branches look abandoned, forgotten or not of any use during this period of the season; however, this is not the case.

The vineyard must have a resting period. The upcoming spring weather and the coming growth shows us that in some ways, the resting period for the vineyard is the most important because of the demands that will soon be placed on it.

This basic principle applies to everything God has ordained. The world and everything in it was created in such a way that rest is an important part of the process of life. Not just life, but abundant life.

As Christians we have a hard time understanding, or maybe excepting this part of God's plan. If we are not constantly on-the-go for God, then something is going to be left undone.

The truth is, the world will not stop turning if you do what God wants you to do and rest sometimes. Rest in Him and His peace will come.

I used to think that if I wasn't in the thick of things, spiritually, then I wasn't doing enough for God; that God had some how shelved me because of something I had done wrong, since He had a lot of people to choose from.

I began to feel like the branches looked in the winter season, alone, left out in the cold, abandoned. But this is a necessary process in order to be more productive when we are in the season of producing fruit.[2]

---

2 This statement does not address the issue of how sin can temporally interrupt our communication with God.

God created the world in six days and on the seventh He, what?

It is recorded in Holy Scripture that Jesus often times went to be alone in a quiet place to rest or pray.

A time of rest always makes the time of producing spiritual fruit all the more effective. Even the great missionaries, Otis and Martha Brady took furloughs.

And He said to them, "come away by yourselves to a secluded place and rest a while".
Mark 6:31

"So there remains a Sabbath rest for the people of God. For the one who has entered his rest has himself also rested from his works, as God did from his".
Hebrews 4:9-10

These scriptures are to be taken to the heart of man, because without the "rest" part of life, the growth part can become dangerously compromised.

"Come to Me, all who are weary and heavy-laden, and I will give you rest".
Matthew 11:28

So, go for a bike ride or a walk and look around at the marvel that God has created for you. Listen to the gentle voice of the Holy Spirit as you spend that time alone with your Creator in communion with Him. Thank Him for sending His Son that you might have life and produce fruit for the Kingdom.

Chapter 26

Only the Vinedresser Can Do this Work

The Disciples had various backgrounds. So varied, I often wonder how they got along at times. When Jesus was speaking to them, He always spoke in terms they could all understand.

Consider the lilies of the valley... a man went out to sow some seed... if a man has a hundred sheep and one of them goes astray... Jesus spoke about things they had known all their lives. He spoke to them of the common, the every day, the obvious. He took what they understood in the physical and attached the spiritual to it for a far deeper meaning.

What was something they all understood? Something none of them would have a problem completely understanding? The one thing that twelve Jewish men would have frolicked in as children and maybe worked in as adults? The thing they all partook of more times than they could remember? Vineyards, wine. The disciples understood everything about them. It was part of their culture, part of the very fabric of who they were.

So when Jesus explained to them their relationship in Him and the direct correlation with a vineyard, they understood perfectly; that He was the vine, and they were the branches and God the Father was the vinedresser and it made perfect sense to them.

No one can do the work God does in our lives except Him. He is the one who allows the storms of life to shake everything that can be shaken. He is the one who speaks to us in the midst of that storm and with His word, that storm is over.

Like the disciples, we too have very different backgrounds and this is why he speaks to us as individuals in ways we personally can understand, and He does it in such a way that we know it is Him working.

God has a way of showing us our strengths, as well as our shortcomings, in a way that only He can.

I was teaching a Sunday school class a few years ago and was as prepared as I had ever been for anything I had ever taught. I had taught a similar lesson before and with my new research added, I was ready to see the spiritual eyes of my students open like never before. I couldn't wait for 9:30 on Sunday morning to arrive.

I looked up just before I began to read a passage from the scriptures and noticed the class was packed. This is going to be good, I thought to myself as I began to read. For whatever reason, I couldn't read that passage accurately to save my life. I started over, I misread words; I stumbled along and finally finished. When I looked up, the whole class was staring at me like a deer in the middle of the road staring at the oncoming headlights of a car. Then looking down at my four pages of notes, I discovered I had only brought three of them with me. No problem, I thought, I know this information frontward and backward. As the class went along, I found myself saying things that made absolutely no sense to me whatsoever. I must have lost my train of thought at least five times and then picked up in another part of my lesson. The room seemed to be twenty degrees hotter than it had been when I started. I could not wait for that hour of my life to be over. When

I had finished the closing prayer, the students seemed to bolt out of the class faster than usual. As I locked the classroom door behind me, I felt as if I was leaving the scene of a crime, a crime that I had committed. During the drive home I began remembering all the things I wanted to teach and didn't. I felt like a complete failure.

Later that day, one of the seminary students who was in the class came up to me and said he wanted to thank me for that class. He said that I spoke on the very issues he had been struggling with. He said that Christ had changed his life through that class and wanted to thank me for being obedient in that teaching. He rattled off the issues he was speaking of and I tried to show a look of concern on my face as I wondered what in the world he was talking about. Later in the week, I received a call from another student and she gave a similar response to me about that particular class. I had no idea how to respond to these uplifting praises about the class. The class I couldn't wait to end. I simply said, well, I tried.

Through that one class, God had shown me His love in a new way. When I thought I had completely wasted everybody's time and let God down, He wanted me to see that the work He wants done, no one else could do.

God wanted me to realize how He will and does use us in ways that we may know little about. He is touching people's lives through us that we may not be aware of at all. What I thought was a disaster, was exactly the work He wanted done. God did a work in my life and a work in some students' lives at the same time. The work He did was completely different for all of us and yet it happened simultaneously. Only God can do this kind of work in our lives.

He allows us to fall down and yet shows us that we never fall down alone. God is the only one who can give us the opportunity to produce spiritual fruit in our lives. He has already done the work so that if we abide in the Vine, we will bear fruit unto Him.

C O N C L U S I O N

If I haven't known a labor of love before writing this book, I certainly have after. It will always fall somewhere between my first and last, but it will always be my favorite. Mainly, because of the life that I have come to see through it. Some say a teacher always gets more from the preparation of a lesson than the students ever will and I often wondered if before I finished this book if Christ would return for you and me and the whole point of my research was so that God could show only me these truths. Well, I guess not, now that you are reading it. But, isn't that just like God. To love us to the point of doing whatever He needs to show us His love.

As you might guess, what God has shown me through the work of Aldo the vinedresser has brought me to my knees more than a few times.

It's exciting and sad for me to finish this work and yet I know the vinedresser's work in never finished. If you ever get the chance to visit northern Italy, stop by Ca' Bruzzo winery. Say, Robert said it would be alright. Aldo will be there, but he will be out in his vineyard doing what he loves to do. He will come out of the field once he knows you're there and to him it will be like meeting an old friend. You will know it's him by the way he looks and what he is wearing.

God, the Vinedresser's, work is never finished either. If you feel you haven't had the chance to visit Him, you can say hello right now. Say, Robert said it would be alright. He will be there and His field is not so big that He won't give you His undivided attention. You will know it's Him by the way He looks and what He is wearing.

Part Five

*A*t the close of John chapter 14 in verse 31, Jesus makes the statement, **"Get up let us go from here"**.

There is the indication that Jesus and His disciples left the upper room and walked over the ravine of the Kidron to the garden. As they walked, there is a good possibility they passed one or more small vineyards along the way. It is here, along this walk that Jesus may have spoken the words to His disciples.

Around this time of the season, the branches would have been in full leaf and growing with the speed that mid-spring carries with it. The object lesson would have been as real as anything He had ever taught them. With this possibility in our minds lets look at the verses.

COMMENTARY

1. I am the true vine, and My Father is the vinedresser.

Throughout the history of the Old Testament, the Jewish mind has viewed the grapevine as representative of Israel in terms of their religious beliefs. Jesus didn't tell His disciples that He was the vine, but rather the true vine. The true vine means the genuine vine. Jesus states that His Father, God, is the Vinedresser. The vinedresser is the one who plows and prepares the fields. The vine has been cultivated by the vinedresser and has taken root and the branches must rely on the vine. The prepared soil is God's soil but the branches cannot benefit from the life in that soil except through the vine. This is one way of looking at salvation. Christ, the vine, has reconciled us, the branches, with the prepared soil of God. He has bridged the gap between sinful man and God.

2. Every branch in Me that does not bear fruit, He

takes away; and every branch that bears fruit, He prunes it so that it may bear more fruit.

I believe that as believers in Christ, we as individuals have in us many branches that produce fruit in many ways.

For example, one can visit an elderly person that might be lonely and we can then mow our neighbor's lawn and later smile at a stranger we meet in a café. All three of these possibilities have the potential of God to bring a person to the saving knowledge of Jesus Christ, thus producing spiritual fruit.

Another example would be if a person has three ministries going to reach the lost. If one of these ministries is having no results, then it is entirely possible that the branch, or person's ministry, will end up being stopped or cut off as Jesus puts it.

And by doing so, there is more time available to spend concentrating on the ministries which are producing fruit or, maybe the possibility exists for starting another type of ministry.

Either way, the person ultimately ends up producing more fruit.

Another point; There is not a negative connotation in this verse. Some view it as the vinedresser disciplining or punishing the branches that have failed, but in fact it is a very positive point. God prunes or puts right the branch for His ultimate purpose.

This verse has nothing to do with an individual losing their salvation, because that is entirely impossible once you are in the family of God.

3. You are already clean because of the word which I have spoken to you.

To be already clean in Christ means to have heard the words in which He has spoken, and to have accepted Him as the Messiah. Accepting Christ as your personal savior has cleansed you. In fact, it has washed you whiter than snow.

To clean a branch, the vinedresser does what is necessary for the branch to produce the most fruit and the best fruit.

It may not have to do only with pruning a branch, as we discussed in Chapter fifteen.

4. *Abide in Me, and I in you. As the branch cannot bear fruit of itself unless it abides in the vine, so neither can you unless you abide in Me.*

Abiding in Christ is prayer. Live every day for the cause of Christ. As much as possible, see things around you as Jesus does. Not so much in the physical world, but in the spiritual world. See the lives around you that don't know Jesus as their savior as people who are lost for eternity if you don't do something. I believe this is how He saw the people of His day and how He still sees them today. To abide in Him is to see and feel and live as He did.

Then with that mandate to go in Jesus' name to a dying world: bear fruit. Bear fruit in loving one another. If we don't continually live in Christ we may not be in a position to see as He sees.

5. *I am the vine, you are the branches; he who abides in Me and I in him, he bears much fruit, for apart from Me you can do nothing.*

Without Christ in the center of our lives, it's not that

it is impossible to please God, although that is true, but we can do absolutely nothing spiritually good for the Kingdom of Heaven

6. If anyone does not abide in Me, he is thrown away as a branch and dries up; and they gather them, and cast them into the fire and they are burned.

This burning up is a reference to a person's works. If you put anything in a fire, after the fire has consumed all that it can, the only thing that will remain will be that which was stronger than the fire itself. Anything a believer does when he or she is not abiding in Christ, will be burned up at the judgment seat of Christ. If we do a work in ours or any other's name other than Christ, it cannot last throughout eternity. Jesus once said that Heaven and earth will pass away, but my words will never pass away.

7. If you abide in Me, and My words abide in you, ask whatever you wish, and it will be done for you.

This is one of the great promises of the Bible by our

Savior, if seen in a non-distorted light. If you are abiding in Christ, then you are walking in the power and in the leading of the Holy Spirit. It means you are producing fruit for God. A lot of fruit. The best fruit that you can produce because of the way God is using you. You are making decisions that are based on the word of God and that have eternity in the forefront of your mind. The Holy word of God has found an abode in your life and in your soul. Since this is the case, anything you ask of God will be exactly what He wants you to have even if you didn't ask. Because of this prerequisite of abiding in Christ, that which you ask will be done for you.

8. By this is My Father glorified, that you bear much fruit, and so prove to be My disciples.

Jesus has told us that there is a way to glorify God, a way to exalt and a way to honor Him, even a way to worship Him and that is to bear much fruit. To bear the fruit of advancing the Kingdom of God, by sharing the gospel message of the Savior of the world, to the world. Doing this proves that you are a disciple of Christ, and not only a disciple, but you are an ambassador for

Christ and this Glorifies God.

Our lives should reflect the love that God has for the human race. The harvest of fruit never comes from us. It comes from God and because of Christ it passes through us. Allowing it to pass through us is the proof that we are disciples of Christ.

9. *Just as the Father has loved Me, I have also loved you; abide in My love.*

The love of the Father towards the Son is a love that is flawless. There is nothing that has ever come between the Father and the Son and they have perfect union with each other. There is perfection in this love that can't be fully understood. The Father and the Son do not think alike but rather they are one. They are one in their heart and one in their thinking and nothing can separate their fullness and completeness in one another.

For a reason that partially eludes me, Jesus has made it clear that in the very way God loves Him, He in turn has loved us. With all our faults, frustrations and failures, He still loves us in the way in which God loves Him.

If we dare to come out from the shadow of disbelief
and into the sunlight of the truth about how it is that
Christ loves us, it can free us from every complex man
may create.

STUDY GUIDE

Chapter 1
Seeing Differently

1. Sometimes the very common things around us have
   tremendous spiritual application for our lives
   depending on the way we look at them.
   These are the types of parables Christ used.
   Jesus would take some physical thing that He created
   and attach a deeper spiritual meaning to it.
   We have been able to see the Kingdom of God, in a
   deeper way of understanding through His parables.
2. Describe a time when you saw something in a
   different way and were able to draw from it
   something spiritual.
3. In watching the vinedresser and seeing the intimacy
   he has with the branches, explain how it makes you
   feel knowing this is how God takes care of you.

Chapter 2
Two Types of Vineyards

1. What are the differences in the two types of vineyards?
2. Which one of the two types of vineyards most closely represents the relationship between God, His Son Jesus and Christians?
3. What are the reasons for your answer?

Chapter 3
The Different Ways to Look at a Branch

1. What are the four variables that can change the outcome of the grapes in a vineyard as mentioned in this chapter?
2. Read Jeremiah 29:11
   The vinedresser knows the future of his branches if they are starting to grow tangled with each other. Because of this, he sometimes separates them and puts them right so they will produce fruit in the proper season.
   Give an example in your life when God had stepped in to redirect you, but you were unaware it was Him

until you were able to look back on the situation.

3. How has God helped you in life to where you are sure it was Him?

Chapter 4

Some Branches are Woven Back in

1. There are some times when the vinedresser will purposely put a younger branch next with a older, more established one.

   He sometimes even binds them together for a short period of time until the younger one is strong enough on its own and no longer needs the tie with the older branch.

2. Describe a time in your life when God has allowed you to be put next to a believer that was farther along than yourself spiritually where that person helped you in your relationship with the Lord

3. What fruit grew out of the relationship between you and the older or more mature believer?

Chapter 5
Grafting the Branches

1. What are the three reasons given in this chapter for the vinedresser grafting branches into another vine?
2. Explain what it means to be joint heirs with Jesus Christ in relationship with an already established root system of the vine.

Chapter 6
Why Prune Off Branches
That Produce Fruit

1. What kind of damage can come from a ministry or an individual who has stopped being accountable in relation to other believers?
   The Biblical account of King David is a great place to start.
2. Give an example how doing a little of everything in an average way, instead of a few things well can cause possible problems in our spiritual lives and in that of others.

Chapter 7
You Can Tell How a Root System Is by What You Can See

1. When Jesus said we would recognize a true believer by the fruit we could see, (my interpretation), what was He indirectly saying about that persons spiritual foundation?
2. Give some examples of what can happen if a believer in Christ only spends their time in prayer and Bible study at a church service, rather than a part of their daily life.

Chapter 8
The Drought

1. Has there been a drought in your spiritual life?
2. When Aldo was telling me the story of letting his vineyard go through the drought, did that remind you of a specific time when God allowed something similar in your life?
3. What happened as a result of your experience?
4. If our heavenly Father stepped in every time we had pain or discomfort in our lives, what do you think the result of that would be?

Chapter 9
Branches Need Time to
Produce Quality Fruit

1. We as believers in Christ began to produce fruit quite early in our rebirth. Think of some ways you spoke to others about what Jesus had done for you the first years you had come to know Him and how that would changed today now that you're older as a Christian.
2. Do you witness to others in a more effective way today than when you were younger?
3. If so how?
4. What have you learned through the years in your bearing fruit that is effective?
5. How do you feel God views you in relation to a branch producing just a small amount of fruit?
6. Like me in this chapter, do you find yourself busy doing everything that comes along at your church and not enough time being what God wants you to be?
7. Spiritual fruit is a byproduct of abiding in the Vine. In your own words explain what this means.

Chapter 10
The Vine is Everything To the Branches

1. If a branch is growing, that does not mean it is merely attached to a vine, but rather it is living from within a vine. Explain in your own words what this metaphor means in relation to the Christian and Christ.
2. How is it that we are able to have good works and yet they can be worthless in the eyes of God? 1 Corinthians Chapter 13 holds the answer.
3. What happens to us if we try to show God that we love Him by what we do for Him? Trying to earn His love and respect can cause certain problems in our understanding of God. What might they be?

Chapter 11
As the Branch gets Older The Roots Go Deeper

1. Explain a passage in the Bible that has gained a deeper meaning for you through the years.
2. How have you changed in the light of how you understand and read the passage?

Chapter 12
The Vinedresser Uses Different Techniques In Training His Branches

1. As the vinedresser looks at the individual branches, he sees that they don't all grow in exactly the same way. Because of this, they must be pruned in the way that is best for the individual branch in order to produce the most amount of fruit. Explain how God has allowed a change in your life that ultimately caused more spiritual fruit.
2. In this chapter are you more like my friend or are you more like me as far as in lessons taught? Whichever the case, give some examples of these lessons.
3. Branches that grow intertwined as in this chapter can support themselves for a while. What does this mean to you?
4. What do you think some negative results can be as you look at the Spiritual side of this?

Chapter 13
The Vinedresser isn't in a Hurry

1. Do you have abilities that are seemingly unrelated to what you are doing in your life now?
2. Is it hard to see how God could ever use some of the things you do for enjoyment or employment?
3. Make a list of the abilities that God has given you no matter how insignificant you think they might be. Make another list of your favorite things to do. In looking at these two lists, think of why it is He has given you these gifts and desires. Make an offering to God of all your abilities and enjoyments that He may use them for His glory.

Chapter 14
Some Branches Grow Correctly

1. Do you know of a good example of a branch that has grown correctly?
2. Think of what that person means to you and how God has used them in your life.

Chapter 15
Preparation for the Harvest

1. Knowing that the words spoken here to the disciples and the promises made to them by Jesus are personally made to us as well, how does this make you feel?

Chapter 16
Cleaning the branches

1. Think about some of the techniques Aldo uses in cleaning the branches and compare them to how God cleans us.
2. What are some of the results in your own life from the process of God's cleaning?

Chapter 17
Gathering the Workers

1. Like Aldo who needs all his family to help bring in the harvest, God has made the same call to us for the harvest of souls into His Kingdom. What does this call mean to you as an individual?
2. What does the call to share the gospel with a lost and dying world mean to your study group and to your

church?

3. Do we as believers in Christ view this, working in the harvest fields for the cause of Christ, as an honor or as a burden?

Chapter 18
The Best Wine Comes from the Fruit Closest to the Vine

1. In looking at the gifts that God has given, the greatest is love. Christ is love. In light of this, how can we give love? We know that someone first loved us and that love was, and is, a free gift. We certainly can't earn it, so we certainly can't boast about having it. We can, however pass on the gift that is given us from God. Think of new ways to share this best fruit, with others around you. Not people who can return love back to you but those who you have the hardest time loving.

Chapter 19
The Quality of the Wine Depends on...

1. Have you been put in a situation where it was hard to witness for Christ because of the actions of another believer? How did you handle your testimony in this circumstance?

2. Has your church gone through something similar to what had happened in this chapter? Have you read about this terrible circumstance? What are some of the results of these types of public sins? Can any good come from this from God's perspective?

Chapter 20
Bringing in the Harvest

1. Doing the work that God has commanded us to do sometimes seems to be just that, work. Still there are other times when the work He has us do is quite exhilarating. Explain a time when you were doing something for the Kingdom of God and you absolutely loved doing it.

Chapter 21
The Vinedresser is Always in the Fields

1. God is always working in our lives even when we are not always aware of it.

Chapter 22
Replacing those Supports

1. Have you ever been comfortable spiritually in life and God allowed a change that wasn't so comfortable?
2. How did you react and what was the result?

Chapter 23
The Vinedresser's Name is on the Bottles

1. We as a society have lost the meaning of the word Christian. Let me restate the definition: the word Christian means to be a follower of Christ. To believe what He believes and to be a new creation because of what Christ has done for us. This is what I believe is the meaning of the name. Have you ever done something that has caused the name Christian to be seen in a bad light?
2. Have you done the opposite? Have you done something that has caused the name of Christ to be looked on in a way that was pleasing to the father? Explain how it made you feel in both cases.

Chapter 24
A Healthy Plant can't help but Produce Fruit

1. What does it mean to hold on to Christ?
2. What are the results of abiding in or holding on to Christ?

Chapter 25
A Season of Rest

1. With the concept of this chapter in mind, think of ways you can rest in Christ.
2. Give some practical ways that rest helps you in your daily life.
3. With the common sense answers of how the rest of daily life is necessary, apply those theories to your spiritual life.

Chapter 26
Only the Vinedresser can do this Work

1. God speaks loudly to us through His creation and yet for most of us it's still hard to hear. Try looking at what God has created around you and listen to Him speaking through His creation. Write down what it is you hear or see differently through what He has created around you.

2. Looking at people and what they are doing is a great way to see God in a deeper way. That is the reason

He had you read this book. Try to see God through something else and then explain what you see.

I was standing beside a vine that was around sixty years old during a harvest, looking at a dark purple cluster of Merlot grapes.

I went to trace the branch back to the vine it grew out from and found it not to be the easiest of tasks. Other branches were growing out of them and those branches had grown from still other branches and fruit came from all of these branches.

It became quite clear to me that I couldn't tell which branch was producing which fruit. It's as if, as the years passed, the branches had grown and had woven into a pattern, into a grand unity. It seemed to me that the branches didn't really care, whether you know which branch produced which fruit, but only that they did produce.

As I was standing and looking at that one clump of grapes peripherally, I could see a lot more, so I walked backwards trying never taking my eyes off that one clump of fruit. After ten or so steps, I lost sight of the one clump in the vastness of all the fruit. A few more steps and I would be looking at a huge rolling hill of a lush green vineyard that was covered in fruit. And I thought, how that one clump of Merlot grapes that is so important to the vinedresser, will be harvested in a few hours along with all the other countless clumps when the workers come through. Then they will be mixed all together to create what the vinedresser intended so long before.

The vine is the single source that transfers the needed nutrients to the branches, so that they may continue growing and produce fruit. Without a vine, there are no branches. However, the support that keeps the branches from breaking once the fruit is on the branches is not the vine only, but also the other branches. It's the weaving into the other branches that over time, causes the support structure that enables the branches to hold up the fruit until the harvest. Without this support from the other branches, once the fruit had started to come to fruition, the weight of the fruit would tear the branch from the others and cause even more damage.

The branches that are helping to hold up the other branch with fruit is producing fruit itself and is being held up by the others as well. So, it becomes quite clear that the branches need the other branches. Not only for the fruit alone, but also because if a branch does not have the support of others, the weight of the fruit tears the branch out of the pattern. That tear causes death to the fruit and can do damage to all the other branches it is connected to.

There are a lot of ways to look at a grapevine. One way that helps us see what God has done for us through His son Jesus, is this. In a grapevine, one could say there are four main parts to the plant.

1. The root system
2. The vine
3. The branches
4. The fruit

Christ is the vine and we are the branches.

If you haven't made a decision to make Jesus Christ the Lord and savior of your live you can do it at this very moment. Let me explain it to you.

The Bible says that God loved this world so much that He gave, as a gift, His Son Jesus the Christ, to this world. And that anyone who believed in Him would not go to hell as all deserve but rather have eternal life in Heaven.

Read Christ's words for yourself found in John 3:16.

For God so loved the world that He gave His only begotten Son that whosoever believed in Him would not perish but have ever lasting life.

The Bible says that all have sinned and fall short of the glory of God and that there is none righteous except for God . Jesus came to earth to proclaim the message of truth that He is the way and the truth and the life and no one can go to the Father except through Him. You can make a decision right now to ask Jesus Christ to come into your life, to fill you with His Holy Spirit. If you do then you will pass from death to life, eternal.

All you have to do is first recognize that you are lost for eternity without Christ as the Bible states. This is a confession. And then ask Jesus Christ to give you new life in Him. At that moment all things become new. Does life become easier, probably not. But that doesn't mean you haven't passed from death to life.

Oh, I almost forgot—find a good church to attend.

If you would like to comment on this book, leave a message for Robert or read his latest article then log on to *http://www.robertscottstiner.com*. He'd love to hear from you.

Make sure you get a copy of Robert Scott Stiners next book called *"RESTORATION"* in 2002.

This book is about the restoring power and grace of Jesus Christ. Look at the restoration process as compared to examples of restoration throughout Gods word and how it applies to our lives today.

There are some who have never known the pain of a shipwrecked life. Some who have not became disillusioned in their beliefs. And some who have not hurt others along the way. But for the rest of us and by the grace of God there is:

"RESTORATION"

Notes

Notes

Notes